Work From Home

Teach English Online

Turn Your Life Around

• Whether You Have a College Degree or Not •
• Step-by-Step, How-To Instructions •
• Lists and Reviews of Hiring Companies •

by Andrea Wood

Work From Home, Teaching English Online

Copyright © 2018 by Andrea Wood.

All rights reserved. Printed in the United States of America. No part of this book may be used or reproduced in any manner whatsoever without written permission except in the case of brief quotations embodied in critical articles or reviews.

For information contact : onlineESLjobs.com

Book and Cover design by Eric Shefferman

ISBN-13: 978 -1724944238

ISBN-10: 1724944231

First Edition: August 2018

Dedicated to Lorl Van Zorge, my former supervisor, my ESL mentor and friend.

Acknowledgments:

Thank you to Eric, for tirelessly encouraging me to create, for formatting this book and cover design, for getting up with me at 5:30am and helping me behind the scenes with my classes in China, the interviews, and so much more. Thank you to SGW for always inspiring me to go after my dreams; writing books has always been one of them! Finally, thanks to oetjobs.com for their ongoing support, to Teachers Ana, Carli Ann, Naomi, Kristen, Kristina, and Melody, for their photo-stories, and to Suelen and Vitoria for the cover photo.

TABLE OF CONTENTS

- PREFACE 13
- INTRODUCTION 15
- PART ONE 19
  - START WORKING NEXT WEEK 19
- PART TWO 29
  - FOUR MONTHS TO A BETTER JOB 29
- PART THREE 35
  - ACE THE HIRING PROCESS 35
    - *Add These to Your Resume* *38*
    - *Step One: The Application* *40*
    - *Step Two: Interviews, Demos, Videos* *41*
    - *Step Three: Training/Evaluation* *45*
- PART FOUR 47
  - POLICIES & PROCEDURES 47
    - *Pay Rates* *49*
    - *Fixed vs Flexible Schedules* *50*
    - *Minimum Work Requirements* *52*
    - *Workday Hours* *52*
    - *Free Trial classes* *52*
    - *Student No-Shows* *53*
    - *Teacher No-Shows and Days Off* *53*
    - *Lesson Plans* *54*
    - *Writing Reports* *55*
    - *Software Platforms* *55*
    - *Teacher Ratings* *55*
    - *Pay Incentives/Bonuses* *56*
    - *Pay Frequency* *56*
    - *Unreasonable Policies* *56*
- PART FIVE 59
  - ONLINE SCHOOLS BY TYPE 59

Independent Marketplaces *61*
Don't Require a College Degree *63*
Online and Offline Ed *66*
Academic Subjects in English *66*
Students in Countries Besides China *67*
Smartphone Apps *69*
Languages in Addition to English *70*
Adult Students *71*
Hiring "Non-Natives" *73*
Discriminatory Schools *73*
Non-Discriminatory Schools *74*

PART SIX **77**

23 SCHOOL REVIEWS 77

PART SEVEN **119**

EXTRA HELP TO LAND THAT JOB! 119
Important Interview Tips *121*
Pre-Demo Test Tips *122*
Demo Lesson Tips *123*
Introductory-Video Tips *124*
Demo-Lesson Video Tips *124*
Get Coached for Free *125*
The Importance of Chemistry *126*
More Resources *127*

PART EIGHT **129**

AFTER YOU GET HIRED 129

CONCLUSION **135**

WHAT NEXT?   PASSIVE INCOME! **137**

ABOUT THE AUTHOR **142**

INDEX **143**

PREFACE

Congratulations on taking this step toward either your first job teaching English online, an additional job, or a move with a company better suited for you. This is an auspicious time to find jobs in this market. More online English companies are hiring right now, than those few that aren't. Additionally, new companies are forming every day. **The projected growth rate for this career is 50 percent!**

Why? English is becoming the "common language" in international companies, where co-workers from various countries need to communicate with one another. I've learned this from my adult students in Bolivia, Iran, Spain, and Ukraine, who are working in just these types of situations. Because of this trend, many parents are also buying online English lessons for their children, in order to give them an advantage.

I put together this book because I realized what a huge life-changer this could be for fluent English speakers who really need more income. This also may help people who are homebound but need to work. I also wrote this book for my fellow online English teachers whom I know would like to learn about a lot of the companies without having to work for them all first.

Once you have read this book, send me a message, and I will add you into our Facebook support group. Also, when you get the job, I'd be thrilled to hear the good news! You can reach me at OnlineESLjobs.com.

Best Wishes,

Andrea Wood

Ready? OK, here we go!

INTRODUCTION

Welcome to the world of teaching English online. This book is for people who:

- are fluent in English but have never taught ESL (English as a Second Language) before.
- have taught ESL offline and want to get online.
- have taught ESL online, and either want to switch companies, or want to add more work hours to their schedule.

For the person just starting out, this book gives you step-by-step instructions on what you'll need, and what to do in order to secure a job teaching English online.

For the online ESL teacher looking for better or additional online companies to work for, as well as for the first-timer, this book also gives you lists of 50 schools by categories, and 23 reviews from my personal job application journey. Toward the end of the book you can find an Extra Help to Land That Job! chapter, detailing what you can do to improve your chances of getting hired.

This book also supplies you with online resources, including support groups where you can find people who will help you with advice and interview coaching.

For the First-Timer
Take these two steps toward bringing in your first paycheck:

1. Read the book.
2. Start taking action *as* you are reading it.

The research and opinions I've given in this book are my own. Some of the information indeed could have changed by the time you read this, because online companies in the English-teaching industry, are new and are therefore still evolving. A successful ESL phone app company I was working for just discontinued their online teacher services. I had a review all ready to go, but had to pull it from this book. A year and a half ago, I got my first online job offer, but they had some really tough rules for their teachers, such as letting students book up to one minute before the regular lesson, and an exclusivity contract; so I went with a different company. Six months later, they improved their regulations, to the liking of their teachers. These are just two examples of how fast the players in this industry are adapting. Changes are not unusual among online English companies, as they navigate the waters of this new enterprise.

The online English business, especially in China is booming! It's the perfect time to look for a job in this field.

In making this book, I have done my very best to help you find a job. While what I'm describing pertains to online language schools in general, many of my examples will be related to jobs which teach English online to children in China. However, I've also supplied you with information on schools that teach other languages, schools that teach adults, and schools that teach online to students in other countries.

PART ONE
START WORKING NEXT WEEK

Start Working Next Week

Yes, you can begin working next week, teaching English online. It may or may not be the salary that you'll ultimately want, but it's a start and you will use the experience that you gain from your first job or jobs, to leverage yourself into working for better companies and for higher salaries.

Let's get started!

Whom do online English teachers work for?

- Themselves
- Online English companies/schools

(From hereon in, I will be using the words "schools" and "companies" interchangeably.)

Here are a few main differences between working for yourself, and working for an online company:

WORKING FOR YOURSELF	WORKING FOR A COMPANY
Find your own students	Finds students for you
Reap 100% of net profits	Pays you much less than 100% of net profits
Spend money and time on overhead	Takes care of overhead
Spend time creating your own lessons	Provides the lesson plans (most schools)

Students' Ages

Some companies teach all age ranges, and to people who live all over the world. However, many companies specialize in teaching the following groups:

- Only Children
- Only Adults
- Elementary to Middle School children (ages 5-14)
- Very young children (ages 2-8)
- Students in China

Policies and Procedures

One might think that all online ESL companies work the same, but alas, one would be gravely mistaken! They are all uniquely different, with very different lesson plans, salaries, and rules for their teachers, including rewards and discipline. "Why so different?" you may ask. The Chinese business culture, for example, is so radically different from that of North America, that there has been an evolution in the development of company policies and procedures to find what works for both the Chinese employers and their multi-national employees. In addition, some of the Chinese online ESL companies are also partnering with Canadian or Filipino companies who take care of the administrative side of their school, thereby combining and incorporating even more cultures' company standards and ethics into the mixes. In this way, there's a complex combination of expectations, trials and errors, and learning curves happening, as companies are adjusting their policies to try to make them more palatable for everyone.

Lesson Plans

The lesson plans which online schools supply their teachers with can run the gamut from no lesson plan at all (only providing the teacher with an interface and supply of potential students who can choose to book them), all the way to providing everything a teacher needs, including the platform, lesson plans and sometimes even specific wording for you to say when speaking during parts of the lessons.

Start Working Next Week

For those just starting out, you need:

- To be fluent in English
- A computer or smartphone

Fluent in English

Online ESL teachers come from all walks of life. Some have bachelor's degrees in English or an English-related subject, some don't have college degrees at all, and some learned English as their second language. (For those of you who are multilingual, check out the Teach Languages in Addition to English section.)

Computer or Smartphone

You Will Need:

- **A Windows 10 or Mac Computer, OR a Smartphone**
  For some companies you must have a computer; for others, a smartphone is required. Some companies check out your computer specs to make sure you have at least an i5 or higher processor and 8GB of RAM.
- **Decent Internet Speed** Many companies will direct you to take an online speed test to test your computer's download and upload speeds. When I started teaching online, my computer had 11 mbps download and less than 2 mbps upload. My Internet worked just fine during lessons, although there were other companies that wouldn't hire me because of the speed number. After I started making consistent money, I upgraded my Internet carrier's speed plan. If the Internet is good in your geographical area, you should be fine.
- **Headset** Companies want you to have an expensive quality headset. This means headphones with an attached mic to block out any sound that might come through your

room's wall or window. I have a Logitech headset which cost $20 on Amazon, and it works great.

- **Background** Some companies want a plain white wall behind you, while others prefer something bright, or even busy, in a kid-friendly way, showing colorful letters, numbers and maps.
- **Props** If you're going to be teaching children ages eight and under, get a hand puppet! You can't go wrong. I bought some on Amazon.

Companies Which Don't Require Work or College Experience

These four companies give everyone a chance to apply. italki has a section called Community Tutors, where beginners can get experience teaching. In the following chart, you'll find the names of the four companies, and links to their job applications.

ABC360   abc360.com/Teacher/Teacher/apply
Cambly   cambly.com/en/tutors
italki   italki.com/teacher/application
Pop On gopopon.com, popon phone app

What if my grammar isn't that good?

I highly recommend the URL englishclub.com/grammar and also the YouTube video, "How to learn grammar – any grammar!!!" by EnglishLessons4U – Learn English with Ronnie!

What if I don't have a college degree, a certificate, or experience teaching?

In the next chapter, I provide a four-month plan toward gaining teaching experience, a TEFL certificate, and then, a better job.

PART TWO
FOUR MONTHS TO A BETTER JOB

Four Months to a Better Job

This next strategy sets the stage for you to acquire a better job. You're going to use the next four months to leverage yourself into a bonafide career of teaching English online.

There are two things you will need:

- A TEFL Certificate
- ESL Experience

TEFL Certificate

You can get a TEFL certificate by buying and taking a course. It can be done online or offline, and it takes about four weeks to four months. Prices range from $19.00 to $2,795.00. If you want to have a better understanding of English and of teaching

English, and if you want to work in person, in an international school, I recommend attending a physical school and spending $2,795, and in four to 10 weeks, getting the superior Cambridge CELTA certificate. A secondary option is to get a top-quality TEFL certificate, also at a physical school, which costs around $1,000. **I went to groupon.com and bought an online TEFL course for $36.**[50] It's grueling work, and took me three and a half months; but the sooner you do it, the closer you are to getting a better online job. I recommend International Open Academy, TEFL Express, TEFL Full Circle, and Global Language companies. Their prices range from $19-$89, **with a groupon**, which you can get through groupon.com. (Don't buy the Grammar certification or the TEFL specialization course; you need the one that says TEFL certification.) *Note: While Groupon may state that your Global Language TEFL course is active as long as you finish the course and get the certificate within one year from when you buy it,* **this is not true.** *While it's true if you buy the course at full price, with the Groupon, you must finish the course within six months, or you'll have to pay more to complete it.*

Experience and Training

During these four months, while you are working on your TEFL certificate, teach online at least a little bit, with one of the four schools I suggested. If you can't, then volunteer to teach someone through

Skype or Zoom. In addition, I would highly recommend getting a few months' of *offline* experience under your belt.

Type into a search engine, words such as "volunteer teach ESL" or "ESL volunteer opportunities," with the name of your city. There, you should find libraries and other organizations which need volunteers to teach English to adult immigrants. Usually, the commitment is only for a few hours per week. Some of them put you through a training program, which is free. These experiences are going to make you a better and more confident teacher, as well as add more weight to your resume.

A Note About Teaching as an italki Community tutor: If you can get clients paying you a decent amount, great; but even if you have to charge $4 per lesson to get clients, remember, your goal here is to gain experience in order to get a better job. Use this time to get better at teaching English, and to have something to put on your resume.

Teaching Children

In addition to acquiring experience and a certificate, if you want to teach to children, you may need to get some experience doing just that. It doesn't have to be teaching ESL, and it doesn't have to be teaching. Although these would be preferable, many children's schools will consider you if you have some experience babysitting, caregiving, teaching in an afterschool program, or being a camp counselor.

"My younger students enjoy learning simple English songs, during our extension time, like "The Itsy, Bitsy Spider," which I'm doing here."
Kristen Zajac is an online teacher and a children's author. Her books can be seen at kristenzajac.com.

See this photo in color at onlineESLjobs.com

PART THREE
ACE THE HIRING PROCESS

Ace the Hiring Process

Once you've been teaching ESL for four months or more, and have acquired a TEFL certificate, the amount of better jobs open to you should increase.

"Better" means different things to different people. It may mean working for a company which offers one or more of the following:

- a higher salary
- employers with kinder policies
- no long, after-hours assessments to write
- a more responsive tech support team

This section will help you apply and interview for a better job.

Add These to Your Resume

Experience Teaching Anything

To make your resume shine, add *any* experiences you've had teaching, training, coaching, and/or mentoring to it. Have you taught something to a class, a group or an individual? Have you trained anyone on a job? Have you helped coach a friend for an interview or audition? Have you taken a newbie under your belt and mentored them for a new industry or hobby they wanted to get into? Add it. If you really can't find a way to put it on your resume, perhaps you can mention it during the interview.

Experience Helping Children

(*If you want to teach only adults, skip this section and continue on.*) If you want to work for a company that teaches children, *any* experience that you have had helping children should be on your resume or at least discussed in your cover letter. This includes being an au pair, babysitter, coach, camp counselor, mentor, teacher, therapist, tutor, parent, etc.

Accomplishments and Abilities

Also, add any of the following credentials or skills that you may have:

- A master's degree in TESOL, English or Linguistics
- A master's degree in anything
- A bachelor's degree in ESL, English or Linguistics
- A bachelor's degree in anything
- Some college experience
- Experience teaching ESL
- Experience teaching ESL *online*
- A CELTA or TEFL certificate
- American, Canadian or British citizenship
- A neutral North American or British accent
- Additional languages you speak

If you have two from the list above, you're hirable!

What if I don't have a neutral accent?

I used to have a New York accent (or should I say Noo Yawk?). So, I took an Accent Reduction class, and now I speak with a neutral American accent. And, now I teach people from all over the world how to speak with a neutral American accent.

Step One: The Application

Online English school websites are predominantly there to attract paying students/clients. For some reason, most of these schools have made links to apply for their jobs obscure and almost impossible to find. To save you time and frustration, I spent hours tracking down the best URLs to take you right there, or as close to right there as possible, and printed over 50 of them in this book. When you arrive at the application, you will fill out information such as your name, address, work and school experience, etc. Some applications will ask for a copy of your TEFL certificate and/or college degree if you have one, your CV (resume), and sometimes a cover letter.

Photograph

Many companies ask for a recent photograph. If you live in the United States, this may come as a shock, since in the U.S., it is illegal for an employer to ask for a photograph. But yes, in China and in many countries, they can take into consideration what you look like. Because of this, it's very important that you choose a photograph that reflects how you want to represent yourself: friendly, approachable, and well-groomed.

Video

Some companies also request an introductory video in the application. If one asks you to do this, you may want to make it generic (don't mention the school's name in the video), so that you can submit that same video to *any* company that asks for one. This way, you only have to make it one time. **More tips on this in the Extra Help to Land That Job! chapter**

Legal Identification

Some companies request uploads of your digital TEFL certificate, college diplomas, and your IDs. *Before you send them your driver's license, passport or social security card, in order to avoid identity theft, make sure you first digitally remove your ID numbers off of jpegs of your ID cards.*

I suggest that you create a folder on your computer, and save all resumes, certificates, photos, videos, IDs, etc. in the same folder, to make your life a lot easier, when applying to companies.

Step Two: Interviews, Demos, Videos

When a company is interested in you, the second step is usually either:

- an interview on Skype or Zoom;
- a pre-demo training;
- a demo lesson;
- a request for an introductory video; or
- a request for a demo lesson video.

Note: The interview may be by someone from the school, or it may be a recruiter hired by the school to find and screen teachers for them.

The Interview

The online interview process is like any in-person interview-- almost. When you go to an in-person interview, the potential employer can see your whole form, and because of personal space, doesn't get too close to you. With an online interview, you really don't have to worry about what you're wearing from the waist down (yay, sweatpants!). But your prospective employer is going to be seeing your head and shoulders closer up than he would in person. And, because you are not in their office with furniture, pictures on the wall to look at, space, etc., they're not going to be occasionally glancing around. "All eyes" will be on you! Therefore, I highly suggest that 15 minutes before your interview, you look yourself over on your computer's camera, and see what you look like. Does your background look neat? Is your shirt bunching up or wrinkling? Do you have stray hairs sticking out in a weird way once you put the headphones on? Does your face look oily? Now's the time to straighten your shirt, smooth your hair, and powder your face. *More tips on this in the Extra Help to Land That Job! chapter*

What is the purpose of the interview? The company wants to see if you're 1) sane and 2) have a pleasant personality. They may ask you questions about your past experiences. Whatever you do, don't remind them that it's on your resume, "As my resume states…" No, no, no; that's rude. Just pretend they don't have it, and tell them a little about yourself. They may ask you "What if" questions. "What would you do if your computer stalls; how would you keep the students from getting fidgety as you fix things?" "Have you ever had the experience of a student not understanding a lesson? And how did you handle it?" They might ask you a grammar question. (Not many, but a few companies give you a multiple-choice grammar test during the application period, or after the interview.) If you're not feeling confident in your grammar, study at englishclub.com/grammar, or at a similar type of website.

Pre-Demo Training and Test

Some companies that have their own platform, train and test their applicants on how to use their software's teaching tools. Examples of features may include screen-sharing, drawing lines, typing words on the lesson screen, giving out digital rewards and more. Some companies train you by having one of their people meet you on video-chat for a session or two. Others provide you with instructional texts and videos. They may give you anywhere from an hour to a couple of days of access to practice, before the pre-demo test. Once you've passed this step, they will schedule your demo lesson. Other companies don't have a pre-demo phase, and go straight to the demo lesson. (If they use a public platform such as Zoom, they'll expect you to figure out how to use the Zoom tools on your own time.) *More tips on this in the Extra Help to Land That Job! chapter*

The Demo Lesson

The demo (demonstration) lesson is sometimes called a "mock lesson" because you are teaching to a pretend student, a staff member pretending to be a child. Other companies actually give you a real, paying student. Either way, the company will usually email you the lesson a day or so in advance, so that you have time to practice before the big day. If you go onto YouTube, you can usually find teachers giving tips on how to succeed at their company's demo class.

One skill that is really important for you to quickly develop before your demo lesson for a children's school, is TPR. This stands for Total Physical Response. It's a teaching method that guides children to use physical movement, to connect their speech and motor skills, improving their recall. *More tips on the demo lesson, in the Extra Help to Land That Job! chapter*

Video Requests

Some companies aren't ready to meet with you yet, and so after receiving your application, they request for you to submit a video introduction.

Others may ask you to make a demo lesson video. Some want you to just read a book to the camera; others, to a puppet or a friend pretending to be a child-student. Still other companies ask to see a video of you teaching an actual child whose first language is not English. (In this case, make sure you get permission from the parents to submit a video recording their child, or just the child's audio with the camera turned off.) ***More tips on this in the Extra Help to Land That Job! chapter***

Step Three: Training/Evaluation

If a company offers you a position with their online school, and you decide to take it, usually the next step is training. Typically, you are given a lesson plan and some time to practice. Then a trainer observes you teach them the lesson online, and then evaluates your performance.

A third training option, which is rarer, is that some companies hire you with a probationary clause.

You teach for a while, receive feedback, are expected to improve. You're paid, and then after teaching anywhere from a couple of weeks to a couple of months, you are told whether or not you are officially hired.

"It is truly amazing to teach across the world. My headset allows me to talk to my students, sing with my students, and feel that I am next to them at that moment." **Melody Parnes is an online teacher and coach for aspiring teachers who would like to work for VIPKID.**
   Email mellowyellody59@gmail.com

See this photo in color at onlineESLjobs.com

PART FOUR
POLICIES & PROCEDURES

Policies & Procedures

Job = Pay + Work Hours

With any job, you want to know how much the pay is, how many hours you must work, and what is required of you to get the job done. Below is a list of the many components that make up an online English school's system, as well as their policies and procedures.

Pay Rates

Schools pay their teachers anywhere from $4 to $23 per hour, base pay (not including bonuses). If you live, for example in India, $4-$10 per hour is livable. Generally, if you live in the United States, for example, you could live on $10-$20 per hour to depending on where you live and how many hours you work (taking into consideration that, for example, a three-bedroom apartment in McAllen, Texas rents for less than a studio apartment in New York, New York). Some companies will negotiate with you, while others pay everyone the same salary.

Fixed vs Flexible Schedules

Some Schools Run on a Fixed Schedule

Being on a fixed schedule means that you've committed to teach for this company for a certain period of time (a month, semester, year, etc.), and that the school has booked your time slots for the same days and hours, every week, with the same students, for that time period. The school doesn't guarantee that they can book all of the slots that you've committed to, or that a class will not be cancelled (if a student drops out); and generally, you don't get paid for the slots that aren't booked. **Exceptions:** Because it's difficult to book lessons from a second company into empty time slots squeezed in between booked time slots that your main company left you with, a few schools "buy you out" or give you "subsidy pay." This means they pay you for hours you've opened, whether you have a class or not. This way, they are committing to you that they value your time, and when they do find a student for you, you will be available to teach that student. Pay for the empty slots can range anywhere from a few dollars, to the same amount you'd be making if you did have a student.

Some Schools Run on a Flexible Schedule

Unlike with the fixed schedule, this type of school usually doesn't book students for you; the students' parents do. When on a flexible schedule, teachers usually click open the time slots they are available to work. Some schools allow you to close time slots you've already opened, as long as a student hasn't booked them yet. This is really convenient, because if plans come up for you, and you don't have a student booked anyway, then you can close it and do something with your time. The school may have a rule as to how much in advance you're allowed to close an open slot. And some schools don't allow you to close a time slot after you've opened it, even if a student hasn't booked it. Also, some schools have mandatory time slots that all of their teachers must open and keep open.

Flexibly-structured schools tend to have more work hours available than fixed-structured schools. Working for two schools, one fixed and one flexible, may be a great combination for you.

Important Note on Scheduling...

Remember to check your work schedule on the school's website, to make sure your time slots haven't changed! Each school has a different rule as to the latest time a student is allowed to book a lesson with you; it could be anywhere from 24 hours in advance, to as little as one minute before start time. If you miss a booked class, they will either give you a warning, or penalize you.

Minimum Work Requirements

Some companies require a minimum quantity of days or hours that you must be available for work. Some require you open specific "peak" time slots that you must be available to work.

Workday Hours

Peak hours for children in China usually means Chinese after-school hours. Depending on where you are in the world, it could mean getting up very early in the morning to teach. For example, I begin teaching at 6 am, my time, to children in China at 6 pm, their time. When Daylight Savings Time ends, it's 5 am, my time, but still 6pm, their time.

Depending on the company, their students' time zones, your time zone, and your preferences, you could generate a work schedule, from morning through the night. The operational hours of online schools for children in China run the gamut from only Monday through Friday, 7pm-9pm, all the way to practically 24/7, for both children and adults.

Free Trial classes

All of the schools that I know of provide free promotional lessons, referred to as "free trials" or "promos," in order for potential students to try out a class, and see if they like it. Some schools teams of teachers: one which teaches the regular classes and one that teaches promo or free trial classes. Other schools give all of the teachers both regular and free-trial classes. Because the schools don't make money from giving away free classes, but still pay teachers for teaching them, they are investing in your teaching abilities to make the new students want to buy classes. If this happens, some schools give you $5-$8 of bonus pay.

Student No-Shows

A no-show refers to a student who was booked for your time slot, and is absent, but never contacted the school to cancel the lesson. Most companies pay you something for your time, ranging from only the first 10 minutes of your class (and then you can leave), to 50% of your salary, to 100% of your salary. Some schools allow you to leave, after a certain amount of time, while others require you to stay for the entire time slot. A late cancellation works the same way as a promo, but for some, it's when a student cancels less than an hour before the lesson; for others, it's cancelling less than 24 hours before the lesson.

Teacher No-Shows and Days Off

If a teacher is absent without calling in because of a technical problem or family emergency, takes a day off without adequate advance notice, falls below a certain rating, misses seeing and therefore showing up for a newly-booked class, or something else unfavorable, some schools give warnings before firing if it happens too often. Other schools dock some of their teachers pay or bonus pay that they've earned but have not yet been paid. Remember, although you're at home, to your employer, you are *at work*. Expect a similar reaction from them as you would a boss at a job location outside of your home.

Lesson Plans

Online English schools' lesson plans vary. Some companies hijack random American picture books, such as Dr. Seuss. Others use American children's educational material designed for native English-speaking children, such as McGraw-Hill Education's Wonders program. Still other schools buy or rent their material from a standard ESL children's program, such as Longman Express. But many of the up-and-coming schools are now creating their own lesson plans, with presentation slides; quite a few, have animation. They generally come with their own trademarked characters, who tend to be children, animals or lovable monsters or aliens with whom the students identify and enjoy encountering in each lesson.

Writing Reports

Some schools require that you write or fill out a report or assessment (also known as "feedback," "memo," and "evaluation") on how each student did in each class, each day. That takes up time, and some schools pay for that time, while most don't. Many schools also require that the assessment is submitted to them within a certain amount of time, and if it is not, you will not get paid for that class.

Software Platforms

Some schools have their own platforms on their own websites, and everything you need is there. Others have you download their software onto your computer. Still, others use their presentation slides on a public video platform, such as Zoom.

Teacher Ratings

Some schools have the students rate their teachers from one to five, or with one to five stars after each lesson. Some of these schools take away classes from their teachers, or give out warnings if the teacher falls below a certain rating. Some of these schools give out bonus dollars if you attain or maintain a certain rating.

Pay Incentives/Bonuses

Some schools give their teachers bonus pay if the teacher shows up for every class; shows up early; refers an applicant whom the company winds up hiring; books a certain amount of classes and/or completes a certain amount of hours within a certain period of time; or succeeds in turning a trial-lesson student into a regular student.

Pay Frequency

Depending upon the company, you will get paid anywhere from a few days after each lesson, to a month after month of lessons. So, yes, it may take almost two months to see your first paycheck. There are also companies which pay every two weeks.

Unreasonable Policies

Some online English companies demand unreasonable things from their teachers. Arriving 20 minutes early to class; writing hour-long student reports; no drinking water while teaching; showing Internet speed test results daily; no working for other companies, receiving weekly evaluations on their teaching, and being docked pay for classroom Internet problems, are some I've heard of. If any of these happen, switch companies.

POLICIES & PROCEDURES 57

Online ESL teacher Ana Marfeo, on creating the right lighting for online teaching:

"I had to take quite a few pictures before finding balance between the right amount of light, background, and position in front of the camera, to make a stronger presence as an online teacher. Found out from my peers' evaluation that my lighting was just too weak. I ended up buying a new camera to help. And it did help. Now I use the exact same lighting as before, but with more efficiency." **Ana can be reached at anapaulamarfeo@hotmail.com.**

See this photo in color at onlineESLjobs.com.

The next two sections of the book give you information on over 50 schools that are hiring. Get out your notebook, and start making a short list of the schools to which you would most like to apply!

PART FIVE

ONLINE SCHOOLS BY TYPE

Online Schools by Type

As much as I want to tell you *everything* about each company, there are so many companies, that I can't possibly know it all. Because these companies are constantly fine-tuning their policies, curricula, and school systems as they evolve into this fascinating and growing market, some of the details I shared could very well have changed by the time this book is published.

I've provided lists of 50 schools in categories to save you time. And, because these schools make it difficult to find their application pages, I've spent hours tracking them down and printing them here, too.

Independent Marketplaces

The following companies are mostly for adult clients who can book lessons for themselves with any of the teachers working through said companies. As a teacher, you would get a profile page where you can fill out a profile, and post a photo and video introducing yourself, then fill out your availability on your profile's calendar. You create your own lessons and tailor them to your individual students' needs. You are paid per lesson; at the completion of each lesson, the student's money is released to your account on your profile page, and then it's up to you to transfer the funds using PayPal or something like it.

Cambly
cambly.com/en/tutors
italki
italki.com/teacher/application
NiceTalk
(phone) nicetalk.com
Palfish
Palfish phone app
Pop On
Popon phone app
Preply
preply.com/en/teach
Verbling
verbling.com

Don't Require a College Degree

Here are companies which, at the time of this writing, don't require a college degree. If you have a TEFL certificate and some relevant experience, you have a good chance of procuring an interview with at least one of these:

ABC360   abc360.com/Teacher/Teacher/apply
ALO7   tutor.alo7.com
Acadsoc   acadsoc.ph/recruit/jobs.aspx
Best Teacher   areyoubt.com/howtoapply
Cambly   cambly.com/en/tutors
DadaABC   dadaabc.com/teacher/job
EnglishUp   englishup.com/teach-for-us
Fluentbe   email contact@fluentbe.com

Schools Which Don't Require a College Degree (continued)
Dialect
dialectapp.com/teach
English Ninjas
englishninjas.com/signup/tutor
HelloKid
tutor.hellokid.com
italki
italki.com/teacher/application
Landi (degree preferred, not required)
teacher.landi.com
Magic Ears (will accept with B.A. in progress)
t.mmears.com
Nicetalk
nicetalk.com
OKpanda
okpanda.com
Palfish
Palfish phone app
Pop On
gopopon.com, popon phone app

Rype App
rypeapp.com/teachers
Qkids (but must be enrolled in college)
teacher.qkids.net/apply
Tutlo
en.tutlo.com/apply
SayABC (for three-month contracts)
t.sayabc.com
Skyeng
study@skyeng.ru
The TalkList
thetalklist.com/en/tutor
Tutoring360 (but must be enrolled in college)
tutoring360.net/apply-to-teach
TutoringLab
en.tutoringlab.net/29
Verbling
verbling.com/teach

Online and Offline Ed

These are brick and mortar English schools that recently began to teach online as well.

English First Englishtown.com/teachonline
Fluent City fluentcity.com/teach-with-us/online
Rosetta Stone 540-236-5164
Berlitz survey.berlitz.eu/bvc/form_A.php

Academic Subjects in English

LatinHire (uses Spanish and Portugese) latinhire.com/en
Landi teacher.landi.com
Sprout/Whales sprout4future@rouchi.com

Students in Countries Besides China

Douroosi   Middle East   douroosi.com/home/find-a-tutor/be-a-tutor
English Gang   Thailand   portal.englishgang.com/register
Fluentbe   Poland   email contact@fluentbe.com
LatinHire   South America   latinhire.com/en/
Learnlight   Many countries in the world   careers.learnlight.com
Learnship   Many countries in the world   Email jobs@learnship.de

Mentorphone   Korea   email mentorphone@gmail.com
Open English   South America with plans to expand into Europe   openenglish.com/en/
Skyeng   Russia   study@skyeng.ru
Vivaling   The World   vivaling.com/join-us-as-a-coach
Voxy   The World   voxy.com/about-us/careers/

Smartphone Apps

These companies use phones instead of PCs, and almost always teach adults. Rates are usually per minute, and from what I hear, average to about $10 per hour:

English Ninjas
englishninjas.com/signup/tutor
NiceTalk
nicetalk.com
OKpanda
okpanda.com
Rype App
rypeapp.com/teachers
Palfish
Palfish phone app
Pop On
Popon phone app

Languages in Addition to English

Fluent City (Spanish, French, Italian, German, Arabic)   fluentcity.com/teach-with-us/online
italki (all languages)   italki.com/teacher/application
LearnLight (all languages)   careers.learnlight.com
Learnship (13 languages)   email jobs@learnship.de
Lingoda (English, German, Spanish, French)   lingoda.com/en/become-teacher
Rype App (nine languages)   rypeapp.com/teachers
Verbling (all languages)   verbling.com/teach
Vivaling (English, Mandarin, Spanish French, German)   vivaling.com/join-us-as-a-coach

Adult Students

Cambly   cambly.com/en/tutors
Dourousi   douroosi.com/home/find-a-tutor/be-a-tutor
English First   Englishtown.com/teachonline
English Ninjas   englishninjas.com/signup/tutor
First Future   firstfuturejobs.com
Fluentbe   email contact@fluentbe.com
Hujiang   teach.hjclass.com/career-job.html
italki   italki.com/teacher/application
LatinHire   (Must know some Spanish or Portugese)   latinhire.com/en
LearnLight   careers.learnlight.com

Learnship
email jobs@learnship.de
Likeshuo
likeshuo.com/recruit/teacher
Lingoda
lingoda.com/en/become-teacher
Mentorphone
email mentorphone@gmail.com
Open English
openenglish.com/en/careers/teachers
Rype App
rypeapp.com/teachers
Skyeng
study@skyeng.ru
TutorABC
recruit.tutorabc.com/program
Verbalplanet
verbalplanet.com/tutorregister.asp
Verbling
verbling.com/teach
Voxy
voxy.com/about-us/careers/

Hiring "Non-Natives"

Here is a regularly-updated list, by Bret Tutor, with companies that hire good English teachers from any country. https://oetjobs.com/non-native

Discriminatory Schools

At the time of this writing, USA Sishu advertises in Chinese, on their website that "Native American white people teach you." In November, 2017, QuQuABC, replied to an applicant with, "Sorry, just be notified that we don't hire black people. Your accent is quite good, though. Maybe you can try…" and suggested other ESL companies. I asked a HelloKid recruiter if they hire black teachers; the reply was, "We'd like to, but actually, facts show that it's hard to sell, so we don't hire black teachers." A friend asked Waijiaoyi if they would hire black teachers, they said, "Probably not." I've also read a post by a biased recruiter that didn't represent their company's sentiments, and I know of a company that has hired teachers of color, but their client-school in China refuses to use them. Also, there is a discriminatory issue regarding native English speakers who are not from native English-speaking countries.

Non-Discriminatory Schools

I can happily report that the best companies don't discriminate against color or age. I've read posts by teachers accusing schools of not hiring them for biased reasons, and I've checked on companies and found photos and videos of their teachers of color and advanced age. It could be very hurtful when we try our best and a company rejects us. It's happened to me, and I've wondered if it was because I'm 53 years old. But I did research and found out that nope, the company has hired older women; they just didn't want me. Although I get offers 80% of the time, 20%, I don't. This is a major reason why I wanted to help others, by writing this book. I'm hoping that all of this information will save you time and money, help you cultivate great interview techniques, and find you companies that you like and that are most likely to hire you.

The rest is up to you. You can do it!

"I love my 'classroom.' I created my background from some fabric that was my grandmother's. Pink is my favorite color, and I feel that it brings a nice pop. Behind the fabric, I have a large, magnetic oil drip pan attached to the wall; I can attach so many props to it. I created my name plate using trusty ole Powerpoint and a fun font I downloaded. The popsicles are just one set of many external rewards I have created for my students." **Carli Ann McClure is a coach for VIPKID and can be reached at carlimcclure@yahoo.com. Her referral code is 056ZD4.**

See this photo in color at onlineESLjobs.com.

PART SIX
23 SCHOOL REVIEWS

23 School Reviews

I really lucked out. I love the company I work for. They have limited work hours, and so I went on a search for a second company to work for also. That's how I wound up applying for and interviewing with so many companies! And I've become friends with a lot of the recruiters along the way.

In the following reviews, I share with you my personal experiences with these companies, taking you through my application or hiring process with each one of them, as well as what I *personally* liked and didn't like.

Please bear in mind that I have friends who love working for companies that I didn't; and vice versa, some friends have had negative experiences with companies that I personally love. So, take what you read with a grain of salt, and please do your own research as well.

The companies that I've reviewed for this book are:

1. 51Talk
2. 61kidz
3. ALO7
4. BlingABC
5. DadaABC
6. Fast School
7. First Future
8. Gogokid
9. Golden Voice English
10. HelloKid
11. Hujiang
12. Landi
13. Learnlight
14. Magic Ears
15. Qkids
16. SayABC
17. Seer English
18. Sprout

19. TutorABC

20. UUABC

21. Verbling

22. VIPKID

23. Vivaling

51Talk was one of the first Chinese companies I'd heard of. They started out with a teacher base in the Philippines; once the company became financially solvent, they created a second website and began hiring native English speakers. The lesson plans revolve around an illustrated bird named Eric, but recently I saw a lesson plan with lovely illustrations of children, so this may be in the process of changing. This company runs on a flexible schedule. Starting pay is $15/hr for native English speakers, and $10/hr for non-natives. Teachers are required to write student assessments.

What I personally like (but you might not):
- 51Talk provides an extensive amount of work hour options, so long as you also teach their minimum requirement of peak time slots.
- The lesson slides have good solid lessons.
- There is an extra-flexible schedule option, if you stand by for up to one minute before someone books a lesson, you can teach a lot of classes.

- In addition to 1:1 (one teacher to one student ratio) classes, 51Talk now also provides group classes for children, as well as 1:1 lessons for adults, which pay more.

What I personally don't like (but you might be OK with):
- The illustrations show only white children.
- For the regular classes, a student is able to book a lesson in as little as 10 minutes before start time.
- Once a teacher has scheduled themselves as available for a time slot, they can't close it, even if a student hasn't booked the slot yet.
- Teachers could be docked $4-$16 of their salary if an emergency or mistake causes them to miss a class.

Personal experience: I interviewed with 51Talk a year ago. The first part of the training included a series of instructional videos, and a couple of live group training sessions through Zoom. The training was good, and the trainer was very nice, but I didn't feel anywhere near ready to work because although they showed us how around their platform, they use various interfaces depending on the student, and we didn't actually enter any of them. I was concerned that I wouldn't even find them on my first day. Secondly, they gave us a link where all the lesson plans links could be found, but didn't teach us or test us on finding specific ones. Also, on my first and second days of work, I woke up very early in the morning and sat there, with no bookings, waiting in case someone scheduled a lesson up to one minute before (keep refreshing the page) and got paid nothing for my time. Lastly, during training I learned that 51Talk had an exclusivity contract at the time, and I had just gotten hired for a company that I preferred. 5ltalk.com/na

61kidz supplies online English teachers to early-learning brick and mortar classrooms in China. The students have their regular school teacher in the classroom with them, and the online English lesson is televised on a huge monitor, for all of the students in the class to see. The online ESL teacher uses a lot of animated expressions and gesturing as they interact with the whole class. The lesson is bookended by 61kidz's short "intro" and "wrap-up" videos, featuring 61kidz's cartoon mascot, Super Ant.

What I personally like (but you might not):
- Their service is a very innovative concept.
- There are no minimum day or hour requirements.
- Starting pay is $25 per hour, with incentives for bonuses.
- The company has sent some of its teachers to visit China; videos can be seen on YouTube.
- The company is growing.
- For us North American teachers, this school gives us the opportunity to work at night instead, Mondays-Thursdays. (For teachers on other continents, it may be in the middle of the night.)

What I personally don't like (but you might be OK with):

- Their theme song, "Super Ant," sung by their mascot of the same name, and taught to the children to sing and dance to, is unintentionally a little provocative for preschoolers, reminding me a little too much of The Runaways' "Cherry Bomb" (particularly Dakota Fanning's version in the movie).
- A video lesson in "New York food," introduces hamburgers, coke, ice cream and pizza as desirable food, with the effervescent sounds as they watch sparkling coke filling up in a glass, and the prettiest ice cream showered with rainbow sprinkles. The 30-second "wrap up" cartoon shows Super Ant flying through the sky, scoring pizza, hamburgers, ice cream and soda.

Personal Experience: I love the rep! He's very positive, open-minded, friendly and caring. We've chatted a few times over Skype, and have made plans to chat more about the company and where it's going. It's definitely a consideration. **Note: Going to press, I have not heard from this company in a while. If it went out of business, try three other companies with similar structures: SinceWin, Class100, and Orange Talk.** 61kidz.cn

ALO7 is a large company, which means they are hiring a lot of teachers. Pay begins at $16 per hour, but teachers are given bonuses after their first 50 hours of work, and again once they've accumulated 500 hours as long as its within their first year. Actual schools (not individual students), book the teachers. Lessons are 25 minutes long. ALO7 requires its teachers work a minimum of 6 hours per week.

What I personally like (but you might not):
- ALO7 has its own platform with fully animated lessons.
- The company has won an educational award.
- Its main characters are cute creatures with names and their own voice-overs for the students to identify them by.
- In addition to regular weekday hours, ALO7 has 12 hours available on Saturdays and on Sundays (China time).
- The school pays 100% for no-shows, as long as the teacher stays in the virtual classroom for the session.
- ALO7 sends their top-voted teachers to visit China.

What I personally don't like (but you might be OK with):
- The school penalizes by docking several dollars, or removing promised bonus money, for reasons such as taking time off without enough notice; but also gives the opportunity to file appeals.
- Both the individual students, and the schools which book the teachers, rate the teachers. (The schools' ratings are important enough to affect your standing; the students' ratings are not.)

Personal experience: I applied, interviewed, did a demo class, and got accepted, but they are very strict about download/upload speed, and said I'd need to upgrade before they could hire me. I did, and I was hired. They scheduled me for a training, and they use WeChat for support; I messaged a friendly hi, with a question, and I received a two-word reply. I went for the second demo/training which is called a "75-minute Experience Session". Teachers need to prepare two lessons, and it came with a list of things you'd be assessed on, including posture, neat appearance, using props, and making the children (aka the trainer) laugh. I spent a lot of time practicing for this. When it came time for the appointment, I met my trainer in Zoom, gave a friendly hi, and was about to introduce myself, when he cut me off, and asked me to go to a different webpage, other than the lesson. I was taken aback and said I didn't know how to get there. He didn't respond, but continued looking at me. I remained calm and asked if this was part of the test. He said that this wasn't a test and then began to quickly tell me the new website name—which was Chinese—and spell it out for me in Roman-style letters. I typed them in, as he corrected me. Once I got onto this new page, I saw that it was my scheduling/class access, etc. page, which of course was blank, since I was brand new. He drew rectangles with the Zoom tools on different areas of the blank page, and quickly said, "To the top-left you'll have your last classes, to the top-right, your reviews. Now if you have a 'One-to-Three,' blah *blah*, but if you have a 'Mini,' blah blah *blah*." I stopped him and he looked annoyed. I asked, "What is a Mini?" He replied, "A Mini? You thought I said a 'Mini'? I said 'a Many.' If you have *many* children in the class." "Oh," I tried to understand. "So 'a Many' is the expression you use to refer to lessons with many students?" "Yeah," he said and kept going. At this point, I, then and there, unshared my screen, and ended the interview. I said I didn't want to work for a company who treated their employees this way. He responded that he does a hundred of these a day and that's why he gets right down to it, and why he goes quickly. He instructed me to reopen my window to continue. I said no, but thanked him for the opportunity. tutor.alo7.com

BlingABC has had a lot of money poured into it. Good things are anticipated. They don't have an English website for teachers, only a Chinese one for clients, so you must go through an outside recruiter to apply. Classes are 40-minutes long. Pay is $12-$18 per 40-minute class.

What I personally like (but you might not):
• In addition to regular weekday hours, BlingABC has 13 hours available on Saturdays and on Sundays (China time).
• The lesson plans are very good. Its slides had illustrations along with structured questions and answers, directed for singles and groups of students.
• They pay bonuses to weekend teachers and substitute teachers.

What I personally don't like (but you might be OK with):

- They require you teach four days per week.
- Most of its teachers don't have full schedules yet.
- There are tech support and Internet issues.

Personal Experience:
The recruiter was very nice, and when she learned that I was looking for only weekend work, she found another school for me. recruiting@blingabc.com

DadaABC

This fixed-schedule school requires at least two days per week and two hours per day. Pay starts at $16/hr.

What I personally like (but you might not):
- The company's staff books your students for you; so you have a regular, set schedule.
- Lessons are booked one day or more in advance.
- In addition to regular weekday hours, DadaABC has eight hours available on Saturdays and on Sundays (China time).
- Dada does subsidy pay where you get paid 50% for any of your open slots that don't get booked.

What I personally don't like (but you might be OK with):
- Students rate you after each class, from one to five hearts.
- You're paid in terms of Chinese currency, so your payrate in your country's dollars may fluctuate.
- Teachers are required to write up student assessments.

- The demo lesson was from a random Dr. Seuss-type book, although recently I saw that they might have switched to Longman Express, much better.
- Taking a day off requires a minimum of 20 days advance notice, and they dock you 10% of your pay if you take off before then. I've been told they will work with you, but I've read teachers' posts to the contrary.
- You must give 30 days' notice when you quit, or they will withhold your pay.

Personal Experience: DadaABC requires proof of North American or British citizenship before hiring someone. Once I got over the fear of emailing my social security card and state license to a stranger in China (I whited out the numbers), the recruiter gave me a quick, private lesson on how to use their platform. The recruiter and I became fast friends, with common interests. I had some questions about the company, such as, "How much advance notice does a teacher get that they have a new class scheduled?" I was told that she didn't have the answer, and that I couldn't be in touch with the person who knew, until I did the demo class and passed it. So, I did the demo class, which was reading the advanced-children's picture book, One Cent, Two Cents, Old Cent, New Cent, to a real student. I passed, and then they emailed me the contract. I wasn't crazy about the contract (see "What I personally don't like"), or their lesson plan at the time, so I declined. Search: dadaabc apply

Fast School is quite interesting. I was originally told that classes contain 20 children, each online in their own homes, but five of the twenty kids are onscreen and visible to the teacher. The other 15 students are observers; and for each lesson, Fast School circulates on-screen students, so that eventually, all of the children have the opportunity to participate. Fast School also has a YouTube-type show, where they air some English teachers' recorded lessons to their audience.

What I personally like (but you might not):
- The pay starts at $30 or $40 per hour, depending on which type of lesson you teach.
- I really like their lesson plans! They are simple, with photographs depicting the vocabulary that they are teaching, along with structured sentences for the students to speak. There was a lot of thought behind this, in order to make sure that the children understand a word's concept; sometimes they provide two different photographs, in order to show two different definitions of that particular vocabulary word.
- The character illustrations included Chinese children.

What I personally don't like (but you might be OK with):
- The hours are pretty minimal, so if you are teaching for 40 minutes per day, you are making $20 per day.
- You can't see or hear your students.

Personal experience: I emailed and interviewed with the company. I downloaded TeamViewer, and their tech guy came into my computer by remote and checked its speed and specs. I then met with a trainer through both TeamViewer and WeChat; he took me through their YouTube training video. The odd thing, was, there was no audio in the training video, as he explained he didn't have time to add that to it yet. But the *really* odd thing was that while I had been told that five kids would be pulled up onto the virtual stage for me to see and give personal attention to, they instead now have it so that only *one* student will be pulled up and tutored, and... there will be no audio *and* he will be wearing a puppy mask filter so I can neither hear them nor see them, while I am asking him to repeat a vocabulary word and responding with, "Great job!" I turned it down until they fix this. Email apply@fastschool.cn

First Future

runs on a flexible schedule. They named it Flexi, because they also recruit online teachers for offline Chinese schools, and that provides teachers with their Fixed Schedule. They have some interesting work-hour options, too. You can work four consecutive weekdays; or you can work an overnight marathon on the weekends, with two one-hour breaks.

What I personally like (but you might not):
• The company seems very flexible with work hours; if you can't work one of the two schedules mentioned

23 SCHOOL REVIEWS

above, they are willing to negotiate another schedule with you, depending on what you have in mind.
• Pay starts at $13-20 per hour.
• Students don't rate the teachers.
• They pay 100% if there's a no-show in one of their Fixed classes.
• In addition to regular weekday hours, First Future has 11 hours available on Saturdays and on Sundays (China time).
• First Future gives $2-$3 per hour bonuses for perfect attendance and punctuality.
• Although you make a demo lesson video for each school they submit you for (for the fixed schedule), you get paid for it.
• The Chinese schools on the fixed schedules have buyouts; you have guaranteed hours and are paid regardless if they a class booked for you.
• The monthly bonus pay is up to 1.5% of monthly pay based on teaching performance and attendance.

What I personally don't like (but you might be OK with):
• If a student books a Flexi (flexible) class and then doesn't show, you don't get paid.
• Students can book up to 30 minutes before start time for Flexi classes.
• The supervisors at First Future evaluate their teachers weekly with quality assurance assessments.
• Teachers fill out lengthy after-class assessment forms for each student.
• The administration handles teachers' attendance with an elaborate point system.

- The lessons lack a specific, comprehensive lesson.
- The lessons show white, no Chinese children.
- They require 30 days' notice for you to quit.
- Teachers are posting of bonus pay being partially or fully docked unreasonably. (Examples: for saying "Behave better" to a kid; for missing an optional sub class that started one minute after refreshing the page; for not using TPR with a university student; blamed for students' tech problems)

Personal experience: I was excited by the recruiter's interest in me, and eagerness to fast-track me to the second interview. I needed help figuring out how their interview schedule app worked, and the woman I emailed was a bit rude. The recruiter and I had touched base through video chat while he was on vacation and he didn't have time to answer my questions, but assured me that all my questions would be answered on the website if not at the second interview. The second interviewer was sweet, but didn't know the answers to most of my questions, and kept getting up and leaving her monitor in order to ask someone. They offered me $15 per hour, and I asked for $20. She got up to ask for permission, and came back with a final offer of $18. I was told that $20 was for teachers with master's degrees in TESOL. I was interested in teaching Fixed classes only, but at that time, they were trying to fill the Flexi classes. I got the feeling that those were easier to acquire, and that it would take time for First Future to get fixed-schedule jobs set up with schools in China. I found a great support person named Bob, who called me on skype and answered all of my questions, but I chose not to pursue this. firstfuturejobs.com

Gogokid is a new company. Some teachers from VIPKID, Magic Ears, and Landi have been trying out this company in their spare time. Pay starts at $7-$10 per class, plus possible bonus pay.

What I personally like (but you might not):
• Gogokid pays new teachers $150 if they book and teach three classes in their first 30 days, and another $150 if the parent doesn't give them a low rating.
• There is no minimum-hour or day requirement.
• Lesson plan illustrations show children of difference ethnicities, and fun animals.
• They pay bonuses for increased bookings.
• The teachers run on a "credit score," and get raises for days that their score is at 110-120.

What I personally don't like (but you might be OK with):
• Students book the teachers, so no one at the school is working to fill your schedule.
• Teachers lose points and therefore bonus pay when their credit scores dip from having no bookings in a week, canceling/missing classes, and/or technical issues.
• Some teachers are getting blamed for technical interruptions that are not their fault.
• You're paid 60% for promo class student no-shows.

- Very slow tech support.
- Several teachers have posted that Gogokid hasn't paid them for months and is ignoring their emails.
- Both the students and the school rate the teachers.

Personal Experience: The interview slots were so booked up, that it took me three weeks to find one not at 4:30 am. I really dropped the ball on this one. I had two other interviews that day, and because I had less than a day's notice, didn't prepare well for this one. The interviewer was great, and I did well in the beginning half of the demo, but then I dragged for the second half, and I didn't learn the Goodbye Song. Goodbye, Gogokid! teacher.gogokid.com

GVE **(Golden Voice English)** hires American and Canadian citizens only, and works on the fall and spring semester schedule. Pay starts at $18 USD and $20 CAD. The classes are all fixed, and teachers must commit to a September-February and/or February-August schedule. Their lesson plans are their own, with illustrated slides with some animation. In addition to regular class teachers, they also have teams of other teachers at various times of the year, including standby substitute and promo class teachers. Class sizes range from one to six students, and lesson plans go from Grade 1 through Grade 9.

What I personally like (but you might not):
- The illustrated characters have names and story plotlines, so that the students can relate to them.

• Four of the five human characters are Chinese (one is Chinese-American); the fifth character is a white girl living in China. Their ages correspond to your students ages, so as your students advance in their curriculum levels, they watch the characters grow up with them. The sixth character is a cute little dragon.
• Because classes run on a fixed schedule, teachers generally have the same students for a semester.
• The lessons are a great combination of vocabulary, structured dialogue, games, story time, and semi-structured conversation.
• There is no student report required.
• There are no ratings.
• They pay you for your training, after you've taught a certain number of classes.
• In addition to regular weekday hours, Golden Voice has 4 hours available on Saturdays (China time).
• If a student cancels within 24 hours or is a no-show, you still get paid 100% of your salary.
• If a student is a no-show, you can leave after 15 minutes, unless they need you to substitute teach.
• Their support team is excellent.

What I personally don't like (but you might be OK with):
• If you take off a day, giving less than 24-hours notice, three times in one semester, you're fired.
• Some of the lessons mix cultures in a way that is confusing for the students. For example, it's hard to

teach "breakfast" with a picture of bacon and eggs, which has no meaning in the Chinese food culture.
• First month's paycheck is received at the end of the second month.
• Paychecks have been late a few times.
• Canadians start at $20 Canadian which is currently less than their American counterparts.

Personal experience: My application was accepted, and I was invited to do a demo lesson. The interviewer was very down-to-earth, and explained exactly how the school worked, how they treated teachers, what their goals were, and what their policies were. After my demo lesson, she gave me notes on how to improve. In a couple of weeks, I was offered the job, and I accepted. **gveoe.com/tutor**

Note: I don't give out my referral code unless I've met with you via video chat, and I recommend you. You may contact me for an appointment.

HelloKid is a school running on a flexible schedule structure, and they require that their teachers commit to four hours per day, four days per week. Their payrate is $14-$16 per hour.

What I personally like (but you might not):
• The recruiter was a very nice, warm, generous person.
• After teaching for a two-month probationary period, HelloKid buys you out, which means they give

you a full schedule and pay you 100% whether or not you have a student booked as you're standing by.
• They seem to have improved their lessons from random published story books, to a comprehensive, animated system.

What I personally don't like (but you might be OK with):
• HelloKid has a racial discrimination policy not to hire black teachers.

Personal Experience: I can't work for a company that won't hire good teachers because of skin color.
tutor.hellokid.com

Hujiang is a school for both adults and children. They pay their teachers every two weeks. They also have audio-only classes (without video).

What I personally like (but you might not):
• Pay rate is $16-$20 per hour for teaching kids.
• I liked their lesson plan, which consisted of slides with simple illustrations, broken down by Phonics, Vocabulary, Reading and Grammar.
• In addition to regular weekday hours, Hujiang has nine additional hours available on Saturdays and Sundays (China time).

What I personally don't like (but you might be OK with):
• Hujiang's pay rate is $12-$16 for teaching adults.
• Student no-shows pays only 50%.

- Students can book classes up to four hours before start time.

Personal experience: I was very excited that Hujiang teaches adults, because I already have a job teaching children on Chinese weekday evenings, and I wanted to teach additional hours, when adults would be available. The recruiter was nice. She really needed teachers qualified to teach children, and explained that this paid more than teaching adults, and that I could only apply for one group (children or adults), so I let her set up my interview for teaching children, which I figured I could teach on weekends. But I canceled the demo class when I learned that students could book four hours in advance; for my time zone, I'd have to wake up at 3am and sit by the computer for the next couple of hours. This arrangement, however, is ideal for teachers in more convenient time zones. teach.hjclass.com

Landi is a high-end brand under ABC360, and teaches children English, as well as Math, Science, and Language Arts, all in English. (This methodology is referred to as CLIL, for Content and Language Integrated Learning.) It teaches children ages 5-14, and there are two children per class. It requires a minimum of 12 hours per week, usually over a four-day period, and a computer speed of 2 mbps download and upload.

What I personally like (but you might not):

- Landi's lesson plans have sweet, simple drawings of animals and children, with interspersed, animated video clips, with songs.
- They also have audio files of a Chinese teacher's voice, which the English teacher plays for the students. It gives the children behavioral directions in Chinese, such as "repeat after the teacher" and "get ready to sing a song."
- Platform tools move students' screen images onto the lesson screen, and give gold trophy GIF rewards.
- Pay is $18-$22 per hour.
- In addition to regular weekday hours, Landi has Saturday and Sunday evening hours (China time).
- Teachers are provided with a six-month contract.

What I personally don't like (but you might be OK with):
- All of the children in the lessons' illustrations are white.
- Landi rates teachers based on students' comments and teachers' attendance records.
- Landi docks pay for absences and lateness.
- Experience (or free trial) teachers don't get paid for student no-shows, and you could get a new class up to five minutes before start time.

Personal experience: I interviewed for Landi, and after I did my demo class, the recruiter listed the things she liked, followed by things I could have done better. I usually find this type of feedback helpful; however she told me that I should have stated before each new transition what we were going to now learn. How could I have known? Magic Ears, for example, specifically, does not want their teachers to state the new topics. I didn't get the job. teacher.landi.com

Learnlight teaches a variety of languages to adults all over the world. They are based in Spain. Pay is $14-$17 per hour.

Personal experience: The job interview was audio only, via Skype. I didn't get a job offer. I wasn't sure if she could see me or not. As nice as the interviewer was, the conversation felt awkward. Secondly, I believe that this company gives preference, understandably, to teachers who are bilingual or multilingual. careers.learnlight.com

Magic Ears runs on a flexible schedule. Teachers are starting off with fewer classes than they'd like, but expect to have more as time goes on. Classes hold one to four students. Minimum work requirements are 10 hours per week

What I personally like (but you might not):
• It pays $18 per hour, with bonus incentives that could add up to $22.
• Their lesson plans use some animation (moving letters and words), and the platform tools can move the students' images onto the lesson screen.
• In addition to regular weekday hours, Magic Ears has four hours available on Saturdays and on Sundays (China time).

What I personally don't like (but you might be OK with):
• Parents book the teachers.
• The lesson illustrations featured two children, both white. They were also a bit bizarre; the one used as "Mom," was clearly a teenage sister, wearing a high ponytail, a crop top, and poised with attitude.
• Their platform's tools don't include text, so you can't type out any words for the students.

Personal Experience: Magic Ears requires "bouncing-off-the-wall high energy types. I sent in the online application and was turned down. I checked with a friend who works for Magic Ears, who checked, and saw that I was sent the default rejection email. He sent me the interview invitation. I prepared, interviewed, did the demo lesson, and was not offered the job, but was offered free a training session and the chance to reapply. I took the training, then reapplied. I again received the default rejection email. Again, my friend went into the system, and sent me the invitation to interview. I practiced on a friend, giving her smiles, cheery hellos, thumbs up, high-fives, yay!s, and digital rewards; then I retook the interview/demo class, doing everything the trainer told me to do. I again did not get accepted: "…you're a great teacher…but your energy level was not very high…" My friend on the inside inquired, but was not permitted to view my demo lesson recording. Another friend of mine, who is a very bubbly teacher, also did not get accepted, and they wouldn't tell her why. t.mmears.com

Qkids

(formerly known as Funbulous, formerly known as JiuQu) has a very original design: the lessons are almost entirely made up of animated gameplay. Teachers' schedules include both regular and standby classes. You work on a flexible schedule, where you give in your availability weekly. They expect you to work a minimum of eight hours per week.

What I personally like (but you might not):
• Qkids has its own platform with full animation and voiceover in its lessons.
• Its main characters are cute koala and monkey families with names and voice-overs for the students to identify them by.
• The platform can move the students' video screens into the lesson.
• The lessons are interactive, and use tons of game play.
• The platform has loads of video GIF rewards to give out, such as diamonds, royal crowns and Spiderman masks.
• If you need to take off for a last-minute sick day, they tell you to feel better and remind you to get rest.
• In addition to regular weekday hours, Qkids has five hours and 40 minutes available on Saturdays and on Sundays (China time).

- Pay is $16 per hour, with ongoing opportunities for bonuses as well as priority scheduling.
- They pay you for your training.
- If there's a student no-show, you get paid 100%.,
- If there's a student no-show, you can leave after 10 minutes.
- You can take a day off, giving 24 hours notice.

What I personally don't like (but you might be OK with):
- They schedule everyone for some standby classes, in case they need a substitute teacher. If the regular teachers show up, and you don't have to teach, you get half pay.
- I found the attitude of some of the lesson plans, a little bizarre. The monkey and koala kids tease each other. The parents have an annoyed or sarcastic tone when speaking. In one lesson, the kids whine that their house is smaller than their neighbors'. In another, students learn "peed" and "pooped."
- Students rate the teachers from one to five, and if their rating dips below a 4.75, the teachers get warnings that they will be scheduled less. (From what I hear, that doesn't really happen.)
- If there's a no-show, you get the default 4.75 rating added into your average.

Personal experience: After receiving my application, a recruiter emailed me and asked for a video of me reading a children's picture book, as if I were reading to a child. I made and sent this in. I was accepted, and then was asked to sign up on the WeChat app in order to communicate.

From there, the recruiter sent me links to download the Qkids platform and a Google spreadsheet, to schedule my pre-demo appointment. She said she would place instructional videos and texts on how to use their teaching software in the platform for me, and I'd have 24 hours to study before studied my pre-demo appointment. But she didn't send it until 11pm that night, and expected me to take the test the next day. I insisted on getting at least 24 hours, like she said, and she complied. The recruiter then tested me on my ability to use their interactive tools, and the many lesson-games; I passed. She then introduced me via WeChat, to the demo-class trainer, also a very nice person. I did my demo class, passed that, and I then *thought* I was hired. The demo-class trainer asked me when I can teach a trial class, and I assumed it was a free trial class. Nope, it was actually *my* trial, haha. You teach a lesson to real students, and get paid for it. I received notes for improvement, and then my trainer wanted to know when I could teach *another* trial class. I asked her how many trials I had to go through, and she said "Five." After teaching the third, I took another job I was offered. But I do really like this company. *Note: Naomi is a Qkids demo-lesson coach. Use her referral code Naomi3947 when applying. Contact her at naomi.keenan@aol.com.*
teacher.qkids.net/apply

SayABC is an offshoot of VIPKID. It has its own platform, with up to four students per class. Lessons run from Monday to Saturday, 6pm-9:10. Two-day paired "homerooms" are as follows: Monday with Thursday, Tuesday with Friday, Wednesday with Saturday, also Saturday with Sunday. Your computer speed must be 20mbps, although some recruiters are OK with 10mbps. Pay is $15 per 40-minute class, but bonuses can bring it up to $21.

What I personally like (but you might not):
- No minimum work days or hours required
- No rating the teachers
- The lesson plans are cute.
- Embedded in the slides, are click-buttons to play songs, roll animated dice, and reward students with animated GIFs.
- The lesson's illustrated characters are four, colorful goofy monsters with names, and six children.
- Each time you teach nine consecutive homeroom classes with perfect attendance, a bonus raises your salary for those nine classes, from $15 to $21 per class.
- If the support team asks you to sub a class that you weren't booked for, you're paid $22 per class.

What I personally don't like (but you might be OK with):
- Their platform's tools don't include text, so you can't type out any words for the students.
- If you're 11 hours late with your feedback, they dock part or all of your bonus pay.

- The children characters are all white.

Personal experience: The interview and demo lesson were combined, and I passed. Next was an orientation. Lastly, I taught an evaluation class. I passed, and received a job offer. I accepted. **Update:** After teaching a couple of one-student classes, one day I had two students; and when I wrote feedback right after class, it wouldn't submit. I tried about 30 times over 24 hours, emailed screen pictures to them via two emails plus Skype, asking for help. Some fellow teachers also had this problem and fixed it by restarting their computers. I finally got help this morning from tech support, after the 11 hours elapsed, and they explained that I had to switch tabs and fill out all students first instead of hitting submit for each student's feedback. But despite all my effort and proof, (and no instructions explaining how to do this), they insisted on docking some of my bonus pay, (didn't tell me how much), which means I'd make $15 or so for eight upcoming homeroom classes, instead of $21. It's not fair or worth it to me, so I quit. t.sayabc.com

Seer English

has filled their quota of non-native teachers, and now wants to do the same with native teachers.

What I personally like (but you might not):
- Pay is from $16-23

- In addition to regular weekday hours, Seer has hours available on Saturdays and on Sundays (China time).
- They don't require a minimum amount of work days or hours.
- If a teacher calls in sick, they don't penalize for it, and they express caring.
- No rating the teachers
- The lesson plans are unique in that they're simple and focused on helping the students get in as much English-speaking time as possible.
- They use illustrations with a lot of details, and a charming overlay of animation and sound effects embedded in the slides.

What I personally don't like (but you might be OK with):
- The cover of the lesson had a bad grammar mistake, "Different kinds of Traffics [meaning, "types of transportation"] in New York City." There were two other mistakes, and I'm used to mistakes in other schools' lessons, but usually they aren't words that don't exist (there is no "traffics," as traffic is not countable, and doesn't mean vehicles.)

Personal experience: Seer's application requires submitting a partially scripted video introduction. Mine was accepted, and during the combination interview and demo lesson, I was offered the job. I loved the interviewer. She was very present and treated me as if she were talking to a friend. I was happy and accepted the offer. During the interview, she'd told me that teachers are compensated for student no-shows; but when I returned for training, the trainer told me that teachers are only paid for the first 10 minutes of student no-shows. So, I walked away from it. Later, she emailed me saying that I qualify for a special program which pays 100% for no-shows; but at that point, I was unsure. t.seerenglish.com

Sprout

(also known as **Rouchi** or **Whales English**) Sprout runs on a fixed, semester schedule. In addition to English, they teach classes in Reading, Writing, History, Math, and Literature, all in spoken English. (This methodology is referred to as CLIL, for Content and Language Integrated Learning.) The school requires being available for a minimum of eight peak hours per week, but I've read posts of teachers who only have two hours per week, and others who have a few schedule. Classes include two to four students. Paid training takes six weeks. The company also has a summer camp in China, and invites their top teachers to come to China! It's a great opportunity to meet your students in real life.

What I personally like (but you might not):
- They pay up to $22 per hour.
- In addition to regular weekday hours, Sprout has 13 hours available on Saturdays and on Sundays (China time).

What I personally don't like (but you might be OK with):

- The lesson plans were from McGraw-Hill's programs. Personally, I find using English material for already-fluently-speaking American children, isn't as helpful for children of the same age who aren't yet fluent.
- Classes are 50 minutes long, and you're not paid per class but "per hour," (50/60 of your hourly rate).

Personal experience: Sprout used a representative or agent to weed out potential teachers; I passed the interview and she set up an interview and demo lesson with a person at Sprout, but I was on the fence because I was very busy at the time; but I would consider this company I've chatted with Lolita the head a few times, and she's very intelligent, and looking for good teachers. Send an introductory video to sprout4future@rouchi.com

TutorABC

Also known as iTutorGroup (*not iTutor*), they teach children, as well as adults in China, Taiwan and Japan. Their pay chart shows salary levels depending on credentials and experience; 25-minute classes pay $6-$11, and 45-minute classes pay $12-$18. The minimum requirement of working is seven hours during peak times, four of which must be on the weekend.

What I personally like (but you might not):
- They have many flexible hours for teaching adults, nearly 24/7.

What I personally don't like (but you might be OK with):

- See Personal experience.

Personal experience: The recruiters and consultants all use the same Skype profiles for messaging, and don't identify themselves; one even let me go on thinking she was someone else when we made plans to meet for the interview. They also kept their cameras off while interviewing and training me; one turned hers on when asked, the other claimed a technical issue. At my interview, I was told I had a mock lesson starting in five minutes in another virtual room. Then, the person didn't show up until 12 minutes late, and that was after I'd messaged her asking where she was. They offered me the job but didn't offer me a rate. When I asked, she said that it's in the agreement and that I wouldn't receive the agreement until after training. We fixed that, but one of them sent me a link for a live training without a date or time, and the next day said oh, the link expired because you didn't use it. And, one of them Skype-called my home, waking me up at 3:45 am. ("Apologies. I thought you are GMT.") The trainer sped through, wouldn't answer my question fully, said she we didn't have time although we had an hour to go, and then she ended my training and transferred me to a supervisor to reschedule my training after I got my question answered. I decided that God does not want me to work for them for whatever reason, because things kept going wrong. But then a recruiter called me and said she got me a new trainer. And the trainer was great. Then I went

to open my schedule, and it wouldn't work. I emailed them and no one replied. After five days, I reached out again and got an email that they decided not to hire me after all. I found out from a friend that I was one of at least four teachers she knew of who were all turned away after being hired during that period.
recruit.tutorabc.com/program

UUABC is a new, promising company, whose classes teaches up to four students at a time, and is planning on adding academic classes to their curriculum. Currently, its school hours are Monday – Friday 5:50pm-7:30pm, and Saturday – Sunday 7pm - 9:15pm, China time. The two types of regular classes are 25 minutes long, and 40 minutes long. Students have a choice of booking only four lessons, or scheduling a half year or a full year of classes.

What I personally like (but you might not):
• UUABC uses Longman Express, based on Hong Kong International School textbooks, which have great illustrations and lessons.
• Their technical support is there in a minute.
• The starting pay is $18-$23 per 40-minute class.
• They pay $15 per hour subsidy for time between classes, and opened slots during peak hours.
• If a student is a no-show or cancels an hour or less before the lesson, they pay you 100% of your salary.

What I personally don't like (but you might be OK with):

- If a student cancels an hour or more in advance, you get paid based on $5 per hour.
- There is no Chinese teacher in the class to communicate to the students if there's an issue.
- If you teach trial classes, they are standby; and if no student books your slot, they only pay you based on $5 per hour, instead of your regular rate.
- The students rate their teachers one to five stars after each class ends.
- A student may book a trial class 30 minutes prior to start time.

Personal Experience: The recruiter was very nice, and I really liked her. She was fine with me only working weekends, and even encouraged me to start out small with only the peak hours and then see how we feel later. Definitely a company to consider. Email teacher.hr@uuabc.com

Verbling has its own video-chat platform, which is used for teaching any language to adult students in any country. There are no lesson plans; that is up to you. Verbling prefers teachers with experience. Teachers create and post videos introducing themselves, and what their lessons and teaching styles are about. Students book whomever they so choose. In exchange, Verbling takes 15% of your profits. There's really not much of a personal journey to share, (I just applied and got in, no interview, etc.) but here's a list of what I like and don't like:

What I personally like (but you might not):
- There is no minimum requirement of work hours, no penalties.
- You set your own hours, and your own rates.
- You receive your pay within a week after a lesson finishes.
- You have a few choices upon how you'd like to cash out your money: PayPal, Payoneer, Transferwise, or credit for taking lessons from a Verbling teacher.
- You can save your lesson plans on their website; making them easily accessible to use again.
- You can set one regular rate, and a discount bulk rate for five or 10 lessons. You can also set different rates for individual students.
- You can create and post courses made up of five or ten lessons.
- You can create discount coupons.
- They publicize you for the first two weeks.

What I personally don't like (but you might be OK with):
- They have an exclusivity contract; you can't work with a similar company, such as italki.
- Students often have problems entering or remaining in the Verbling interface; both teacher and student screens freeze often.
- There is no tech support. You're instructed to email "tech support;" they should reply within one to two business days.

verbling.com/teach

VIPKID was one of the first companies I'd heard of. It goes by a weekly or biweekly schedule, of flexible classes. Pay is $14-$18 per hour, plus bonus incentives.

What I personally like (but you might not):
• Has an extensive amount of work times, 9am-10pm China time every day.
• You have the option to get 24-hours advance for new classes. If you'd prefer more opportunities, you can opt for students booking your class up to one hour before start time.
• Students don't rate their teachers.
• There is no required minimum for work hours.

What I personally don't like (but you might be OK with):
• The lessons are PDF formats containing pages with a few illustrations and a word. The teacher draws a line from the illustration to the correct word, and instructs the student to draw a line, too. Sometimes, the lesson page doesn't supply enough help and so the VIPKID teacher really needs to buy a small hand-held whiteboard in order to demonstrate with a marker how two sounds of the word come together to form a word.
• During the lesson, your reward system for the students is teeth on a smiley face. It's not provided by VIPKID in their lessons; the teacher creates their own smiley face (either out of paper or other material, or drawn on their whiteboard), and draws

a tooth for each letter sound/word/sentence the student says correctly.
- Their platform's tools don't include text, so you can't type out any words for the students.

Personal experience: I was invited to teach a mock (demo) class. I got a negative vibe from the interviewer; the only way I can describe it is, although he was smiling and friendly, I sensed that he was judging me in the back of his mind instead of really being present. When it was over and I asked for feedback, he explained exactly how I should have said and drawn things. He also said that I should have had a real apple with me. I didn't get the job; I highly recommend that you take a coaching session with a VIPKID teacher, several whom you can find in this book's photo-stories, before you attempt the mock class. The coaching session is usually free if you add that person's referral code to your application. Also, I'd recommend buying and using a hand-held dry erase board. I bought one on Amazon for six or seven bucks. t.vipkid.com.cn

Vivaling

provides online English, French, German, Mandarin and Spanish lessons to children 3-18 years old, living in Asia and Europe. Lessons consist of 15, 25, 40 and 50-minute lessons. The shorter sessions are private, while the longer lessons can be private, or can have up to three children in one class. They use Cambridge English resources for lesson plans, plus they give you the freedom to add your own creative ideas using different types of medium.

What I personally like (but you might not):
- It pays $20 per hour plus bonuses.
- There is room for growth, by taking on other positions within the company, such as interviewer.

What I personally don't like (but you might be OK with):
- You pay them for training you.

Personal Experience: After submitting my application, I was invited for a video-chat interview, which was delightful. Then, I was scheduled for a second interview and also asked to submit a video of myself teaching a real child. During the second interview, the interviewer mentioned that after being hired, Vivaling's 120-hour training took 12 weeks, but since I have a master course TEFL certificate, I would be fast-tracked to a 20-hour training over two weeks. I asked if I would be paid for the training, and I was told no, in fact, I would have to pay Vivaling! I believe for those without my level of training, it would cost around $1,000, but for the fast-track, it would cost $475, which she offered to discount to $375. The tuition is referred to as a deposit, because once you have taught 1,000 classes, they will reimburse you the money you spent on the training. This is estimated to take about one year. I wanted to work for this company, but I made it clear that I wouldn't unless I was given a full scholarship.

vivaling.com/join-us-as-a-coach

One More List!

Honorable Mentions, Word of Mouth

Here are six more schools that lately I've been hearing great things about:

Am Class   Email teacherhr@usavip.com
KK Talkee   t.kktalkee.com/info.html
nicekid (also known as 98kid)   Email hi@nicekid.com
PandaABC   pdabc.com/recruit
SinceWin   Email vivianduhuihui@gmail.com
USKid   teacher.uskid.com

PART SEVEN

EXTRA HELP to Land that Job!

EXTRA HELP to Land that Job!

Being Prepared

How does one become prepared for the online interview, demo lesson, and video submissions?

Important Interview Tips

Pick out your clothes ahead of time. Make sure they're clean and wrinkle-free. (I'm not an ironer, so I just make sure I've hung them up ahead of time.) Decide how your hair will be brushed. If I'm having a crazy, flyaway day, I use a tiny dab of Frizz-Ease to tame that.

While I'm teaching, I keep a hairbrush, a lip balm, and some face powder and blush brush within reach, to freshen up in between lessons. This is a good idea to have within your reach before the interview starts, as you're setting up. (I use NYX HD finishing powder in Translucent or Banana, but you could even use baby powder and a cotton ball.)

Sit at your computer and turn your camera on so that you can see yourself the way that the interviewer will see you. Does your background look good? Is your lighting bright enough? As an actress who records YouTube shows on her computer, I'd bought an umbrella lighting kit on Amazon, and they're helpful with online teaching as well. Try on your interview shirt and make sure the color jibes with the background and your chair.

As far as the interview goes, be confident. Less experienced teachers who were more confident have gotten some jobs that more experienced teachers haven't. The interviewer may or may not ask you to tell them a little about yourself, so practice ahead of time what you will say.

Pre-Demo Test Tips

Companies with their own platform will either give you limited access to figure out the tools on your own, or will train you, before they test you. *Take advantage of whatever time they give you.*

Some companies use the public Zoom platform; if this is the case, sign up for a free account at zoom.us, and practice. Free video tutorials can be watched at zoom.us/livetraining.

EXTRA HELP TO LAND THAT JOB!

Demo Lesson Tips

Demo lessons for children's schools will usually include TPR (Total Physical Response method of teaching). I highly recommend you check out the YouTube video, "How to Use TPR in the Online Classroom," by Kristina Garcia (Teacher Tina).

Kristina Garcia is an online teachers' career coach who helps by proofreading your resumes and cover letters, and does roleplay mock interviews to get you ready for the big day. Email her at teachertinavipkid@gmail.com.

See this photo in color at onlineesljobs.com.

There's no reason for you to go this alone. Especially if you're new to ESL teaching, I highly recommend that you get a mentor to coach you. Some of them will coach you for free, because if you get hired, and had used their referral code when applying, they will get a referral fee. Others make videos on YouTube and hope that their tips have helped you and therefore you will use their referral code. **Most of the teachers featured in this book do free coaching.** The companies usually give you 24 hours to a few days to prepare for the demo lesson, so use every bit of time you have to perfect it. Try to arrange for your mentor/coach to meet you online a day or more before the demo test, so that you then have time to practice what they've taught you on your own, or better yet, on a friend. *More tips on this in the Get Coached for Free, and Important Interview Tips sections*

Introductory-Video Tips

In this video, smile, say your name, credentials, experience, what country and city you're from, your teaching style; and end it nicely, saying that you look forward to hearing from them soon.

Demo-Lesson Video Tips

Recording and submitting a video demo lesson can be tricky. I suggest using Zoom, because with Zoom. you can video-record your lesson, share your computer screen, show Google images, a virtual white board, presentation slides, etc., as part of the lesson you give.

Depending on the school's instructions, you might:
- read a book to the camera, as if the camera were a child;
- give a lesson to a friend who is on a different computer and has met you on Zoom, pretending to be a child-student;
- give a lesson to a hand puppet (worked by you or a friend) pretending to be a student; or
- give a lesson to a real child-student. (If it's a real child, make sure that you have their parents' permission in writing.)

Once you've recorded the demo, you may need to edit some middle parts. I edit with an old, free copy of Windows Movie Maker that we found on the Internet; however you may find something else that you're more comfortable with, or your video may not need editing at all.

Lastly, before you make your demo video, make sure that you go over all of the sections in this chapter. Apply these tips, and your video will rock!

Get Coached for Free

It's worth your time to get coached by an experienced teacher who already works for whichever company you are going give a demo lesson to. *Make sure that the person has agreed with you ahead of time that they will meet you for a video-chat coaching in exchange for using their referral code.* I once applied with the reference number of a person whom I later discovered had no intention of meeting with me, only messaging.

If you can't find someone in this book or on YouTube who will meet with you, contact me; I may know a teacher from the company you want to apply to who will coach you.

I said this before, but I repeat: make sure that you don't get the coaching on the same day as your interview. Give yourself time to practice by yourself after the coaching. Also, on the day of the interview, give yourself time (two hours if you can) to relax, as you dress, set things up, and set yourself up for success. Reread and apply "Important Interview Tips" in the beginning of this chapter.

The Importance of Chemistry

While being prepared is your best strategy, I have found that a secondary important aspect of the interview's success or failure really depends upon your interaction with the interviewer, and whether you two like each other. Some of that can't be controlled. The only thing that you can control is your end of it. Be pleasant and kind! The interviewer is a person, and their success also depends on these interviews, too! They want teachers that they can recommend. You can make a new friend from this. And if the chemistry just isn't there, maintain a respectful attitude, and do your best with the situation.

EXTRA HELP TO LAND THAT JOB!

More Resources

Here are some websites and Facebook groups with great people who support each other with advice and coaching to get jobs:

- **Online ESL Jobs** is my Facebook group specifically to help you get jobs.
- **Oetjobs.com** is a phenomenal website with more lists and information on online English jobs than I can mention! Their Facebook group is Online ESL Reviews.
- **Daniel Didio** is a mentor who helps people become online ESL teachers. I recommend his $50 video course and his Facebook group, Hired Online ESL... You can reach Daniel through OnlineESLkidzcoach.com
- **Goodairlanguage.com** is great for learning about different online English companies.

"Puppets are a great way to teach children how to have a conversation; often times, low-level students will not realize that you are asking a question until the interaction is modeled for them. Lighting is extremely important (always dimmer than you think), so I actually have lamps all around me. The laptop is elevated using a physics book (any book will work for this) because the angle allows me more freedom of movement in front of the camera for TPR." **Naomi is an online teacher and coach, and can be reached at Naomi.keenan@aol.com.**

See this photo in color at onlineESLjobs.com.

PART EIGHT
AFTER YOU GET HIRED

AFTER YOU GET HIRED

Once you get hired, the school will put you through whatever their training is, and then you will begin teaching classes. Here are a few things that I've learned the hard way, that I want to share with you in order to make your transition easier.

- Create a before, during, and after class preparation system.
- Create an optional standing desk.
- Take care of your ears.

Your Class Preparation System

You will figure out a system that works best for you, and it will also depend on the school and types of classes you're teaching. Here's an example of a system that I use for one of the schools that I work for:

Before Class

The night before, in my notebook, I write out a list with the next day's timeslots, and corresponding names of students, and lesson. I also go through the lesson slides so that I'm familiar with them beforehand. It helps me figure out how I will teach, and if I want to set aside any props, pictures, and/or videos to help with the lesson. (Different companies are OK, or not OK, with outside media.)

During Class

When class starts, I glance at my notebook just in case I'd written a note to myself. I write down if it's a student's birthday, or if a student had asked me a question that I promised to find out and answer next time. I also check the class order because if I have more than one student in a class, I keep track of whom I called on first the last time, and then I rewrite the students' names in a different order for their next session.

After Class

After each class, I jot in my notebook what I will be teaching the students the next time.

The Standing Desk

Create a standing option for yourself. One morning, when I awoke, I couldn't sit up; my back was stiff from sitting so much! "I need a standing desk in 15 minutes!" My husband quickly stacked two boxes and a step stool on top of my desk. The laptop went on top, and I was good to go. I teach this way now, and it's strengthened my back and legs, and it gives me more energy for the kids when I teach. I still have my chair, and I can always remove the containers to convert it back to a sitting desk. I tend to do half of the class day standing and half, sitting.

Take Care of Your Ears!

Sometimes, I get little kids who have extremely loud voices, or fidget and knock their hands or things into their microphones. Don't put up with anything that can hurt your ears momentarily or give you long-term, permanent hearing loss. When there's a situation where I've lowered my volume as much as possible, and I'm still not comfortable with the noise on the other end, I will pull the headset plug from my laptop, but continue wearing the headset, so that the kids don't know that anything has changed. I'm in a quiet room, so it's usually not a problem.

Also, after having taught for a year with no problem, one day I noticed that my ears were itchy and felt a little clogged. I finally realized that my headphones had gotten too dirty from me throwing them wherever in between lessons, so I bought a new headset. I also began to treat my ears with over-the-counter hydrogen peroxide almost weekly (I apply it as described in Dr. Mercola's video "Hydrogen Peroxide - Simple Trick to Treat the Cold or Flu"), and I've become more conscientious about placing my headphones in a clean place after using them. My ears feel a lot better!

.

CONCLUSION

Well, we've come to the end of this book. But this isn't really a conclusion, because it doesn't end here!

- **OnlineESLjobs.com/FBgroup**
  Once you've finished reading this book, you are invited to join my Facebook group for more support from your fellow readers and me in finding your job.
- **OnlineESLjobs.com/signup**
  Sign up for occasional helpful tips.
- **OnlineESLjobs.com/YouTube**
  Subscribe for occasional quick tips videos.
- **OnlineESLjobs.com/coaching**
  Contact me for my "Land the Job" and "Accent Reduction" coaching packages.

When you land that job, please let me know. I'm rooting for you. You got this!

What Next? Passive Income!

Teaching English online is great, fantastic, wonderful! I love the kids, I love staying home, and I love the process of teaching English. But with teaching classes, we're trading our time for dollars; if we're absent, we don't get paid. So, how does it end? Will we have saved enough for retirement? Enter passive income: money that you continue to make even after your working stops.

Writing this book is an example of passive income. Long after I've stopped typing, people can buy this book, and I can make money while I sleep. If I can write a book, so can you, fiction or non-fiction.

Other examples of passive income include e-commerce, affiliate marketing, blogs and vlogs. And if you were to buy a fast-food franchise, even after you've gone to sleep, your employees are still flipping burgers and filling the cashier with your profits. Probably one of the best ways to create a large amount of passive income in a short period of time (seven years) is joining a network marketing company.

First, I started teaching English online. Then I took on additional online teaching jobs, some from companies, some independent, and saved enough so that if my computer broke or I needed to pay the rent, I had backup. And then I put some away for network marketing.

An example would be Avon, where someone buys beauty products through your Avon page, even while you're sleeping. In a sense, you've bought a franchise, but it's different because buying a franchise can cost between $15,000 to $50,000, with startup costs 10 times that, inventory costs, monthly fees, etc. With a network marketing company, you could begin and invest for $100-$200, and the percent of profits you keep are so much more than a franchise. Plus, legally, you can write off a lot more tax deductions.

Another difference between a franchise, such as KFC, and a network marketing business (also known as MLM or direct selling), is that KFC will interview and sell only a certain amount of franchises in order to not flood its own market. If there were KFCs on every corner, many would start to go out of business. But with a network marketing company, anybody and everybody can join—which means that successful companies eventually become flooded, and then it's harder to become very wealthy being a new member of an already-long-standing network marketing company. So, be wise when choosing. It's better to join a relatively new company that has proven itself and has MLM veterans running it. The one I joined is pretty new, has made huge profits in its first year, and has been created by veteran network marketers who have already built other successful companies in the past.

"Pyramid Scheme!" You will hear people cry this out as if they've seen the Bogeyman. More than one hundred years ago, a scam was created where people would hand their money over to someone else, and then someone would become rich from it. This continued as more and more people became rich, until someone didn't, and lost all their money. Pyramid schemes are illegal and do not involve any products or services. Network marketing on the other hand is legal, and if you know of anyone selling Avon, Scentsy, Tupperware, having lingerie parties, etc., these are all examples of network marketing. The good thing about society's fear toward network marketing is that it keeps the industry from becoming flooded. This industry has made many people extremely wealthy, because the industry has not become too flooded, because of this societal fear.

In addition to choosing a company with a product or service that you find valuable enough to use yourself, you want to look at the specific branch or team of the company that you're considering joining.

Not every team is the same. Now-a-days with the Internet, you don't have to join the team that lives closest to you. The members on my team live all over the U.S., and I've even begun building in Asia. That's another thing, some companies are limited to only a few countries, while others are in many. Find out who the leader at the top of the team you are considering is. Do they have experience? Have they made at least one million dollars in this industry yet? How will they lead and train you and your team? Also, never join a company unless it's possible for you to become wealthier than the people above you in the lineage. That's how it should be structured.

Lastly, what is the compensation plan? Do you only receive commission directly from what people buy from you? Many companies now give four, five, even eight or ten ways to make money, such as commission, team bonuses, check matching and global profit sharing.

Of the thousands of companies built in the last 10 years, only 11 have reached billion-dollar status. Either join one of these 11, or better yet, join a new company that has been created by one of the people who created one of the 11 (The owners of the company I joined created two of the 11; this is their third.) Whichever company and team you choose, feel free to contact me if you have any questions that I can help you with, at onlineesljobs.com/contact.

About the Author

When she's not teaching English or writing books, Andrea acts, writes and produces, helps others make passive income through network marketing, volunteers at housing court. She lives in New York City with her husband.

INDEX

2
24 hours, 103

5
51Talk, 79, 80, 81

6
61kidz, 79, 82

9
98kid, 117

A
ABC360, 63
absent, 53
Acadsoc, 63
accent, 39
adults, 17, 38, 69, 97, 100, 109
Adults, 23
advance notice, 54, 88
ALO7, 63, 84
American, 39, 54, 95, 109
Application, 40
assessments, 37, 56, 87
Assessments, 55

B

Background, 26
being prepared, 126
Being Prepared, 121
Berlitz, 66
Besides English, 70
Best Teacher, 63
BlingABC, 79, 86
bonus, 53, 54, 55, 84, 100, 114
Bonuses, 56
British, 39

C

Cambly, 62, 63, 71
Canadian, 23
Cancellations, 53
CATEGORIES, 59
Children, 23, 38
China, 17, 52, 84, 86, 87, 91, 95, 97, 99, 100, 102, 107, 108, 111
Chinese, 23, 52, 89, 95, 98, 99, 112
coaching, 16, 38, 104, 115, 127
Coaching, 124
companies, 13, 15, 17, 21, 22, 23, 25, 26, 32, 43, 44, 45, 50, 52, 53, 69, 73, 78, 127
Companies Which Don't Require a Bachelor's Degree, 63
credentials, 124
CV, 40, *See* resume

D

DadaABC, 63, 79, 87

days, 44, 50, 87, 96, 107, 113
Days Off, 53
degree, 27, 39, 40, 63
Demo, 43, 44, 123
Dialect, 64
Douroosi, 67, 71

E

English First, 66, 71
English Gang, 67
English Ninjas, 64, 69, 71
English school, 49
EnglishUp, 63
Evaluation. *See* Assessment or Training
experience, 27, 33, 38, 39, 40, 43, 63, 81, 84, 92, 96, 98, 99, 100, 103, 106, 107, 109, 110, 115
Extra Help, 41, 43, 44, 45
Extra Help to Land That Job!, 16, 43, 44, 45

F

Fast School, 79, 89
Feedback, 55, *See* Assessments
Filipino, 23
First Future, 71, 79, 90
Fixed, 50
fixed schedule, 50, 51
Flexible, 50, 51, 80
Flexible Schedules, 50
Fluent City, 66, 70
Fluentbe, 63, 67, 71
fluently, 109

G

Golden Voice, 79, 94
grammar, 27, 43, 107
GVE, 79, 94

H

headset, 25
Headset, 25
HelloKid, 64, 79, 96
hours, 15, 49, 50, 51, 52, 53, 56, 78, 80, 84, 86, 87, 89, 90, 95, 98, 100, 102, 107, 108, 109, 111, 113, 114, 116
Hujiang, 71, 79, 97
Human Resources, 42

I

Important, 51
Incentives, 56
India, 49
Internet, 25, 33
Internet Speed, 25
Interview, 42, 121
italki, 27, 62, 64, 70, 71
Italki, 26, 33, 62, 70, 71

K

KK Talkee, 117

L

Landi, 64, 66, 79, 98, 99
LatinHire, 66, 67, 71
Learnlight, 67, 79, 100

LearnLight, 70, 71
Learnship, 70, 72
lesson, 22, 23, 33, 42, 43, 44, 45, 51, 53, 54, 56, 62, 80, 85, 86, 87, 89, 91, 94, 97, 99, 100, 107, 109, 111, 112, 114, 115, 121, 124, 125
Lesson, 44, 54, 123
lesson plans, 22, 23, 54, 94, 99, 100, 103, 105, 107, 109, 112, 115
Lesson Plans, 54
lessons, 22, 43, 53, 61, 80, 84, 88, 89, 97, 99, 102, 107, 111, 112, 114, 115
Likeshuo, 72
Lingoda, 70, 72
Longman Express, 54, 88, 111

M

Magic Ears, 64, 79, 100
McGraw-Hill, 54, 109
memo, 55
Memo. *See* Assessments
Mentorphone, 68, 72
Minimum Work Requirements, 52
mock lesson, 44
money, 22, 25, 53, 62, 84, 113, 116
month, 50, 56, 96

N

native, 73, 106
network marketing, 138, 139, 142
New York, 39, 50, 107

nicekid, 117
Nicetalk, 64
NiceTalk, 62, 69
Non-Native English Speakers, 73
No-Shows, 53

O

OKpanda, 64, 69
online companies, 16
Online English, 21, 54
Online English schools', 54
online interview, 42
online language schools, 17
Open English, 68, 72

P

Palfish, 62, 64, 69
PalFish, 62, 69
PandaABC, 117
Passive Income, 137
Pay, 49, 50, 56, 83, 86, 91, 99, 100, 103, 105, 106, 114
Pay Frequency, 56
Payoneer, 113
PayPal, 62, 113
Peak hours, 52
penalize, 52, 107
Pop On, 27, 62, 64, 69
Preply, 62
Promo, 52
Props, 26

Q

Qkids, 65, 79, 102

QuQuABC, 73

R

Rate, 49
rating, 54, 55, 103, 105, 107
regular, 56, 84, 86, 87, 91, 94, 97, 99, 100, 102, 107, 108, 111
report, 95
Resources, 127
resume, 38, 40, 43
Rosetta Stone, 66
rule, 51
Rype App, 65, 69, 70, 72
RypeApp, 65

S

salary. *See* pay
SayABC, 79, 105
Scheduling, 51
Seer English, 79, 106
semester, 50, 94
Skyeng, 65, 68, 72
Skype, 42, 100
Software, 55
Software Platforms, 55
specific, 24, 92
Sprout, 66, 79, 108
standby, 80, 101, 112

T

Teacher, 53, 55
Teacher Ratings, 55

INDEX

teaching, 15, 16, 22, 25, 26, 31, 38, 39, 44, 46, 53, 89, 97, 104, 109, 112, 116, 122, 124
TEFL, 27, 31, 40, 63, 116
TEFL certificate, 27, 31, 40, 63, 116
Test, 43
Texas, 50
The TalkList, 65

time period, 50
time slots, 50, 51, 52, 80
time zones, 52, 98
Training, 43, 45
Transferwise, 113
Tutlo, 65

TutorABC, 72, 80, 109

Tutoring360, 65

TutoringLab, 65

U

United States, 4, 40, 49
USA Sishu, 73
USKid, 117

UUABC, 80, 111

V

Verbalplanet, 72
Verbling, 62, 65, 70, 80, 112
Video, 45
VIPkid, 80, 114
Vivaling, 68, 70, 80, 115
Voxy, 68, 72

W

warnings, 55, 103
websites, 40, 127
Wonders, 54
Work Hours, 49
work schedule, 52
Workday, 52
Workday Hours, 52

Y

year, 32, 50, 81, 83, 111, 116

Z

Zoom, 42, 44, 55, 85

www.ingramcontent.com/pod-product-compliance
Lightning Source LLC
Chambersburg PA
CBHW071549220526
45469CB00003B/961